Text by Frederick C. Klein

For the Love of the Cubs

An A-to-Z Primer for Cubs Fans of All Ages

Illustrations by Mark Anderson

Every sports team has a history, but few can boast one as illustrious as that of my team, the Chicago Cubs. Organized way back in the 1870s, they've represented the same city in the major leagues longer than any other club. And while they haven't won a pennant for a while, they won plenty of them in the old days—and they've had great players all along. The spirit and fan loyalty of the Cubs makes them the favorites of many people, a lot of whom don't live in Chicago. I hope that reading this book will help both kids and adults understand what makes the team special.

—Ernie Banks

Baseball brings out the child in all of us, and I can think of no better way to introduce the game to youngsters than with a book that appeals to them while touching childhood chords in adults. *For the Love of the Cubs* is such a book, I think. Its rhymes and drawings evoke scenes from the past of a team whose rich and special history I appreciate more the longer I'm associated with it. I'll be reading this book to my three kids, and getting as much fun from it as they will.

—Chip Caray

"A" is for "Cap" Anson

He managed the team
When baseball was young
And the Cubs were supreme.

ADRIAN "CAP" ANSON JOINED THE CUBS AS A FIRST BASEMAN IN 1876, the year they were formed. He became their player/manager in 1879 and stayed with them through 1897. His teams won six National League championships. He was the first man to get 3,000 hits and is regarded as the best player of the 19th century.

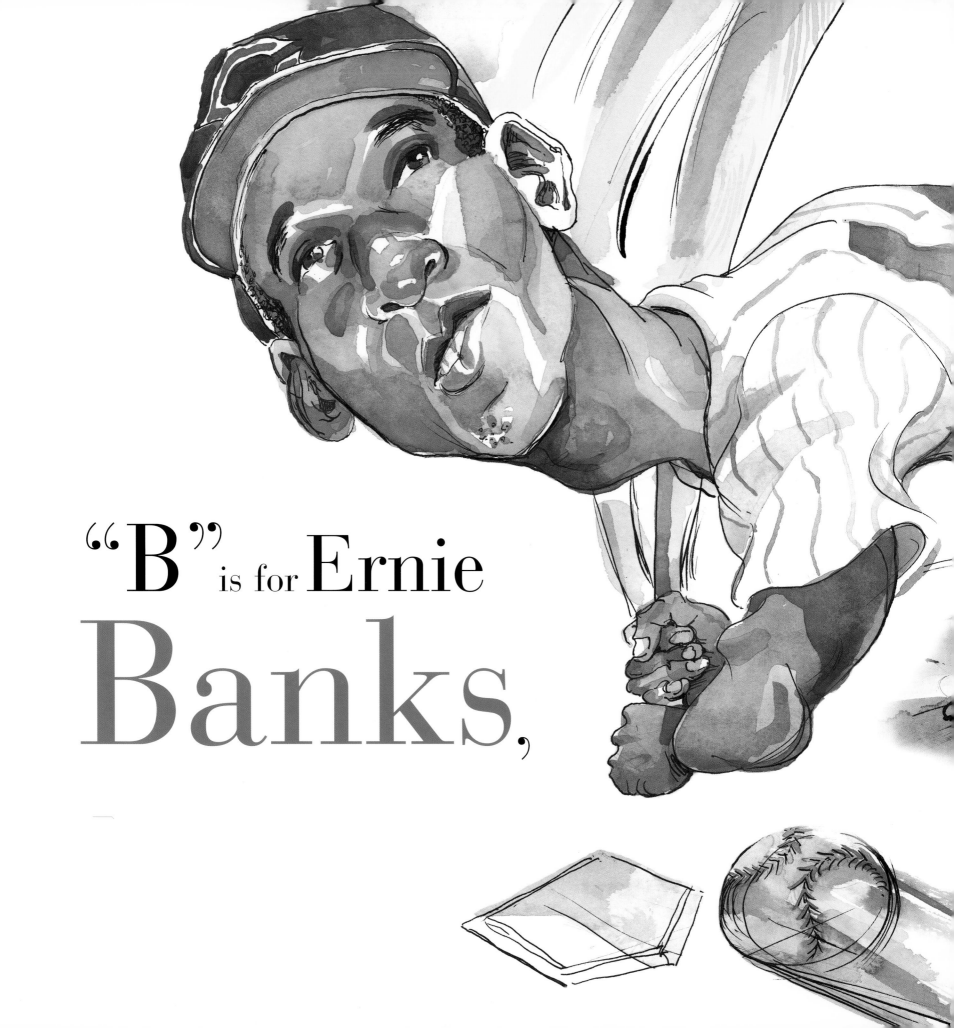

"B" is for Ernie
Banks,

The "Let's Play Two" man.

Number one in team homers,

Number one with the fans.

ERNIE BANKS PLAYED WITH THE CUBS AS A SHORTSTOP OR FIRST BASEMAN FROM 1953 THROUGH 1971.
He's the team's all-time home-run leader, with 512. His cheerful disposition and love for the game made him a fan
favorite. He's a member of the Baseball Hall of Fame, and a pennant bearing his uniform number, 14, flies from a
flagpole at Wrigley Field.

"C" is for Harry Caray

His accounts never dragged.

He made the games fun

Even when the Cubs lagged.

HARRY CARAY WAS THE CUBS' MAIN TELEVISION VOICE FROM 1982 THROUGH 1997. He was a fun-loving man whose colorful language and enthusiasm for baseball made his broadcasts distinctive. A statue of him, leading the crowd in singing "Take Me Out to the Ballgame," stands outside Wrigley Field.

"D" is for Durocher,

Leo the "Lip."

His '69 Cubs

Had a memorable trip.

LEO DUROCHER MANAGED THE CUBS FROM 1966 THROUGH 1972 after having led the Brooklyn Dodgers and the New York Giants to National League pennants. He got his nickname because of his outspokenness and his habit of arguing with umpires. His 1969 team led the league before fading to second place in September.

"E" is for Johnny Evers, who with Tinker and Chance, made a trio that could turn a double play in a glance.

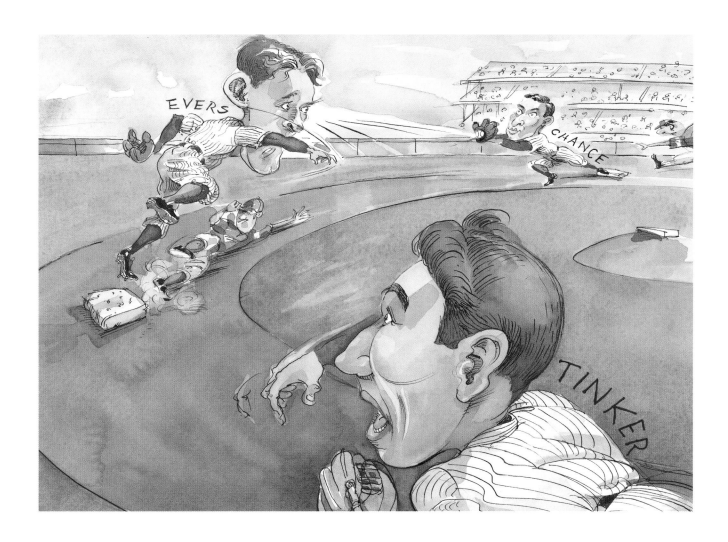

SECOND BASEMAN JOHNNY EVERS, SHORTSTOP JOE TINKER, AND FIRST BASEMAN FRANK CHANCE were the best players on the Cubs teams that won National League pennants in 1906, 1907, 1908, and 1910, and the World Series in 1907 and 1908. All three are in the Hall of Fame. Thanks partly to a poem about them, Tinker-to-Evers-to-Chance remains baseball's most famous double-play combination.

"F" is for the first basemen

Few teams have had better

Than Charlie Grimm, Buckner,

Or Phil Cavarretta.

CHARLIE GRIMM STARRED AT FIRST BASE FOR THE CUBS FROM 1925 THROUGH 1936. Bill Buckner played the position for the team in the seventies and eighties, and led the National League in hitting in 1980. Phil Cavarretta was the league's leading hitter and most valuable player in 1945, when the Cubs won the pennant.

"G" is for Mark Grace

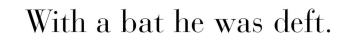

With a bat he was deft.

If they played him toward right,

He would hit it to left.

MARK GRACE WAS ANOTHER OUTSTANDING CUBS' FIRST BASEMAN. He played over 13 seasons, ending in 2001. He wasn't the most powerful batter, but his ability to hit singles and doubles enabled him to get 1,754 hits during the nineties, more than any other player. He was also a skillful fielder who won four Gold Glove awards.

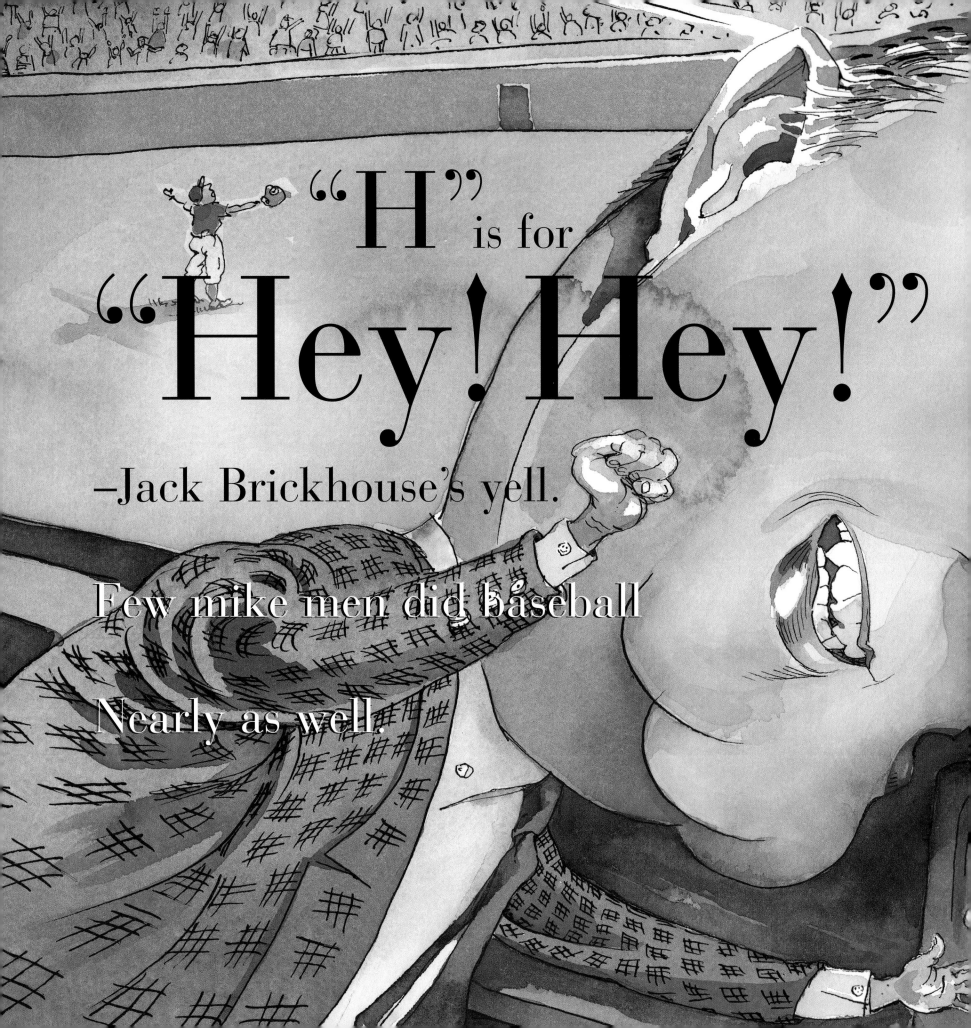

"**H**" is for
"**Hey! Hey!**"
–Jack Brickhouse's yell.

Few mike men did baseball

Nearly as well.

JACK BRICKHOUSE WAS THE CUBS' FEATURED BROADCASTER FROM 1948 THROUGH 1981, a period of 33 years. He was popular with fans because of his cheerful personality and love of the team. He'd cry "Hey! Hey!" when a Cub hit a home run or the team won a game.

"I"

is the word
That's used to mean *me*.
When you're a Cubs fan,
The *I* becomes *we*.

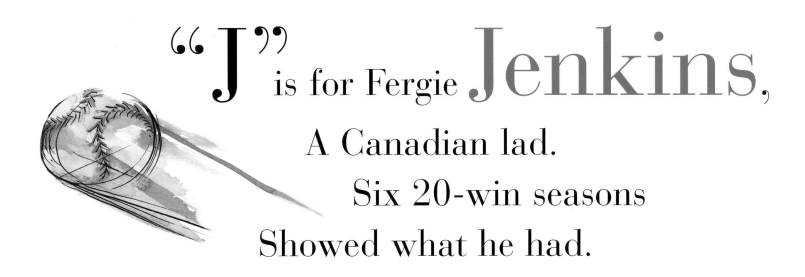

"J" is for Fergie Jenkins,

A Canadian lad.
Six 20-win seasons
Showed what he had.

FERGUSON JENKINS CAME TO THE CUBS IN A 1966 TRADE and won 20 or more games in six of the next eight seasons. The tall right-handed pitcher was traded away in 1974 but returned in 1982 to play his last two seasons in Chicago. Of his 284 career victories, 167 were with the Cubs. In 1991 he became the first Canadian-born player to be elected to the Hall of Fame.

"K" is for Don Kessinger

He was swift, lean, and tall.
The six-time All-Star shortstop
Could go get the ball.

DON KESSINGER WAS THE CUBS' STARTING SHORTSTOP FROM 1965 THROUGH 1975. He was a good hitter, usually batting leadoff, but made his biggest mark with his fielding range and sure throwing arm. He and second baseman Glenn Beckert made up the Cubs' best double-play combination in the second half of the 20th century.

"L" is for left field,

A position for power.

Billy Williams played there,

And Kingman

And Sauer.

HOME-RUN-HITTING LEFT FIELDERS HAVE BEEN A CUBS' TRADITION. Billy Williams (pictured at right) started at the position from 1961 through 1974 and hit 392 homers, ranking third on the team's all-time list in that department. Hank Sauer led the National League in home runs in 1952 while playing left field, and Dave Kingman did the same thing in 1979.

"**M**" is for

Mordecai

"Three Finger" Brown
When a batter came up
He'd sit him right down.

MORDECAI BROWN LOST PART OF THE INDEX FINGER ON HIS RIGHT THROWING HAND IN A BOYHOOD FARM ACCIDENT, but contemporaries said that helped make his curve ball nastier. He won 20 or more games for the Cubs every year from 1906 through 1911, and a total of five games for the team in the 1906, 1907, 1908, and 1910 World Series, three of them by shutout.

"N" is for Bill Nicholson

They called him "Big Swish."

He struck out as often

As a pitcher could wish.

BILL NICHOLSON PLAYED RIGHT FIELD FOR THE CUBS FROM 1939 THROUGH 1948. He got his nickname because he struck out a lot, but he also hit many home runs, leading the league in 1943 and 1944. His eight RBIs led the team during the 1945 World Series, which they lost to the Detroit Tigers in seven games.

"O" is for Billy Ott

He played fairly well.

But the Cubs wished they'd had

The Ott who was Mel.

BILLY OTT WAS A PART-TIME OUTFIELDER FOR THE CUBS IN 1962 AND 1964, his only seasons in the major leagues. He is in this book to show that most big leaguers have short careers, and aren't stars. Of the more than 1,700 players who've worn a Cubs uniform, many played for one season or less. Mel Ott, on the other hand, was one of the game's leading hitters in a 22-year career with the New York Giants, the Cubs' main rival in the twenties and thirties.

"P" is for Milt Pappas

He threw a mean ball.

He missed a perfect game

On an umpire's call.

MILT PAPPAS, A RIGHT-HANDED STARTING PITCHER, won 51 games for the Cubs from 1970 through 1973. He's best known for the game at Wrigley Field on September 2, 1972, in which he retired every San Diego Padre batter he faced before walking Larry Stahl on a 3–2 count with two outs in the ninth inning. He got the next batter for a no-hitter, but just missed a perfect game, the rarest of pitching feats.

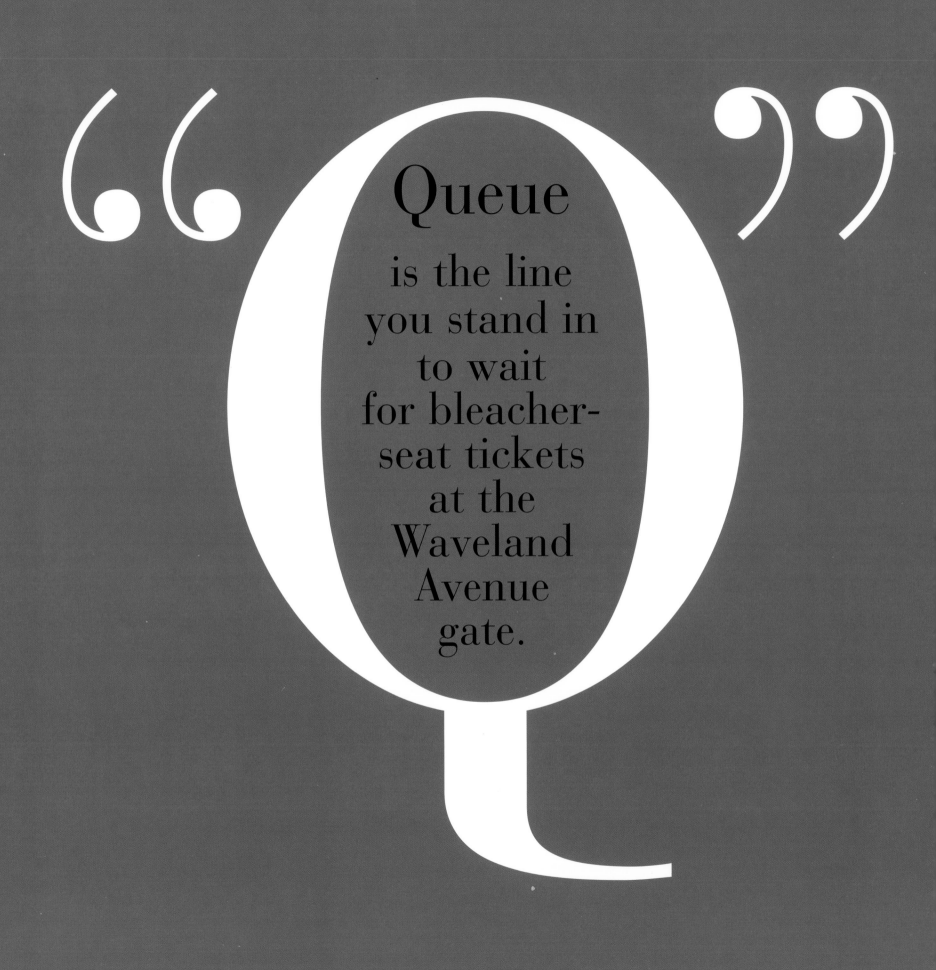

"**Q**ueue is the line you stand in to wait for bleacher-seat tickets at the Waveland Avenue gate."

"R" is for Charley Root,

A pitcher who won a lot.

It was too bad for him

That the "Babe" called his shot.

NO PITCHER HAS WON MORE GAMES FOR THE CUBS THAN CHARLEY ROOT'S 201 FROM 1926 THROUGH 1941, but the right-hander is remembered mostly because Babe Ruth, the great New York Yankees slugger, pointed his bat toward the center-field bleachers in Wrigley Field just before he hit a home run there off Root during the 1932 World Series. Some people question whether Ruth really "called his shot," but the incident is part of baseball lore.

"S" is for Santo
and Sandberg
and Sosa

It's a letter the Cubs

Have sure made the most of.

RON SANTO, RYNE SANDBERG, AND SAMMY SOSA ARE THREE OF THE ALL-TIME GREATEST CUBS. Santo was a nine-time All-Star third baseman in his 14 seasons with the team (1960–1973). Sandberg (1982–1997) was the best second baseman of his era and set a record for home runs by someone who played his position. Sosa, from the Dominican Republic, hit 60 or more home runs in each of three seasons—1998, 1999, and 2001—something no other player has done.

"T" is for "Lefty" Tyler, who didn't give in.
He pitched 21 innings before getting one win.

GEORGE "LEFTY" TYLER WON 19 GAMES FOR THE PENNANT-WINNING CUBS OF 1918, and pitched a six-hitter to win the second game of that year's World Series against the Boston Red Sox. On July 17 of that year he set a team record by going all the way in a 21-inning, 2–1 victory over Philadelphia.

"U" is for "utility man," a fellow who can play
more than one position on any given day.

UTILITY MEN ARE IMPORTANT PARTS OF EVERY MAJOR LEAGUE TEAM BECAUSE OF THEIR VERSATILITY. By moving from position to position they allow managers to change their lineups in different ways. Jose Hernandez, normally a shortstop, played every position but pitcher or catcher for the 1998 Cubs.

"V" is for "Hippo" Vaughn,

With the Cubs in the teens.
His left-handed deliveries
Stirred championship dreams.

JAMES VAUGHN, NICKNAMED "HIPPO" BECAUSE OF HIS LARGE FRAME, was the Cubs' best pitcher between 1913 and 1921, winning 20 or more games five times. In the 1918 World Series he gave up only three runs in three full games, but lost two of those because the Cubs were shut out. Babe Ruth, then a young Boston pitcher, won twice in that Series, which the Red Sox captured in six games.

"W" is for Wrigley Field,

Which is where the Cubs play.
A prettier ballpark
You won't find today.

BUILT IN 1914, THE CUBS' HOME IS THE MAJOR LEAGUES' SECOND-OLDEST STADIUM, behind only Fenway Park in Boston. It was first named Weeghman Park, then Cubs Park, and, since 1926, Wrigley Field, for the family that owned the team. Its ivy-covered walls and lack of advertising signs help make it famous for beauty.

There's an "X" in Jimmy

FOXX

In fact, there are two.
He played with the Cubs
Before he was through.

THE MUSCULAR JIMMY FOXX WAS ONE OF BASEBALL'S ALL-TIME BEST POWER HITTERS, hitting 534 home runs over a 20-year period in the twenties, thirties, and forties. His best seasons were with the Philadelphia A's and the Boston Red Sox, but he also appeared with the Cubs in 1942 and 1944. Many great baseball players have changed teams as their careers were ending.

"Y" is for the year Nineteen forty-five

The last Cub pennant came Before you were alive.

THE CUBS WON THE 1945 NATIONAL LEAGUE PENNANT, then lost in the World Series to the Detroit Tigers. From 1900 through 1945, the Cubs won 10 pennants, a total that trailed only the New York Giants' 12 in their league. They haven't won since, although they won divisional titles in 1984 and 1989, after the league was broken into divisions.

"Z"

is the sound

Someone makes when he snoozes.

A Cubs fan stays loyal

Even when his team loses

Library of Congress Control Number: 2002116947

The book is available in quantity at special discounts for your group or organization.
For further information, contact:
    Triumph Books
    601 South LaSalle St.
    Suite 500
    Chicago, Illinois 60605
    312. 939. 3330
    Fax 312. 663. 3557

Printed in China
ISBN 1-57243-545-3